BIGFOOT
and Other Legendary Creatures

BIGFOOT
and Other Legendary Creatures

PAUL ROBERT WALKER

Illustrated by William Noonan

Harcourt Brace & Company

SAN DIEGO   NEW YORK   LONDON

Requests for permission to make copies of any part of the work should
be mailed to: Permissions Department, Harcourt Brace & Company,
6277 Sea Harbor Drive, Orlando, Florida 32887-6777.

The author is indebted to the International Society of Cryptozoology,
P.O. Box 43070, Tucson, Arizona, 85733. Membership in the Society is
open to anyone interested in the scientific study of unknown animals.

Library of Congress Cataloging-in-Publication Data
Walker, Paul Robert.
Bigfoot and other legendary creatures/by Paul Robert Walker;
illustrated by William Noonan.—1st ed.
p. cm.
Summary: Explores the myths and scientific inquiries surrounding
repeated sightings of such legendary creatures as the
Loch Ness monster, Bigfoot, and the Yeti.
ISBN 0-15-207147-4
ISBN 0-15-201551-5 (pb)
1. Monsters—Juvenile literature. [1. Monsters.] I. Noonan, William,
1923—   , ill. II. Title.
QL89.W34   1992
001.9'44—dc20   90-45856

Designed by Michael Farmer

C E G F D
A C E F D B (pb)

Printed in Singapore

To Devin, the legendary creature in our house.
—P. R.W.

To Shon, whose future is bright.
—W. N.

Contents

Introduction

THIS IS A BOOK ABOUT MONSTERS. Not movie monsters or fantasy monsters or monsters that live under your bed. No, the monsters in this book are large, living, breathing creatures that share our world without our knowledge. Impossible, you say? After all, we know everything, don't we? Consider the story of the okapi.

In 1860 the British journalist H. M. Stanley described how the Pygmies who lived in the tropical rain forests of the Congo (now Zaire) captured a wild donkey called an *atti*. According to zoologists, scientists who study living animals, there were no donkeys in the Congo. The only animal that might be mistaken for a donkey was the zebra, but zebras didn't live in the rain forests.

Almost forty years later, in 1899, a British official named Sir Harry Johnston asked a group of Pygmies about the atti. They told him that it was actually called the okapi and that it was a mule with stripes like a zebra. Sir Harry searched for more information about this strange creature, but the more he found out, the stranger the creature became. It seemed to be a small horse with hooves like an antelope, ears like a donkey, and stripes like a zebra.

Knowing of Sir Harry's interest in the okapi, another colonial official sent him a skin and two skulls of the mysterious animal. After studying this evidence, zoologists realized that the okapi was not a horse or an antelope or a donkey or a zebra. It was actually a short-necked relative of the giraffe! In fact, it was a type of giraffe that existed long before the modern-day giraffe. Today, the okapi is no longer a mystery. You can probably see one at your local zoo.

Now, the okapi is hardly a monster. But it *is* a large, unusual creature that existed for thousands of years without the knowledge of the scientific world. Of course the Pygmies knew all about it, but most scientists don't believe reports from native people. Scientists want cold, hard facts. Fortunately, there are a few open-minded researchers like Sir Harry Johnston who are willing to listen to native reports. And it is these reports that usually lead to the great discoveries.

The okapi is not the only large, unknown animal that was discovered in the last hundred years. Others include the mountain gorilla (1901), the Komodo dragon (1912), and the pygmy chimpanzee (1929). Megamouth, a fifteen-foot shark that represents a completely new species, was discovered in 1976. The most amazing discovery, however, was the coelacanth, a six-foot fish that was caught off the coast of South Africa in 1938. What's so amazing about that? Well, scientists believed that the coelacanth became extinct over 65 million years ago!

In 1982 the okapi was chosen as the symbol of the International Society of Cryptozoology, a scientific organization dedicated to the investigation of unusual animals that are not yet accepted by the scientific world. "Cryptozoology," the study of hidden animals, is a word created by zoologist Dr. Bernard Heuvelmans. According to Dr. Heuvelmans, there may be at least 138 different kinds of large, unknown animals in the world today.

Seven of these mysterious creatures are described in this book. They are among the biggest, strangest, and scariest of the unknown animals—ranging from huge ape-men to giant water beasts to living dinosaurs. Each of these "monsters" has been described by native people and investigated by serious researchers.

The search for unknown animals requires scientific knowledge and methods. But it also requires an open mind and a vivid imagination. This book is a combination of science and imagination. The descriptions and details in each story are based on reports from people who claim to have seen these creatures and on the opinions of scientists and other experts. The characters and events in the stories are the products of imagination. At the end of each story, there is a nonfiction section that tells about the research and scientific ideas concerning the creature.

Perhaps someday you will combine your imagination and your scientific knowledge and find an okapi of your own. Or a Bigfoot. Or a Loch Ness Monster. Or ???

—P. R. W.

THE BIGFOOT

THE FORESTS of northern California are dense and dark. Giant redwood trees tower above the forest floor, blocking the light of the sun. Between the tall trees, gnarled manzanita bushes grow like blood-red demons. The land is mountainous and roads are few. It is the perfect place for a man to disappear—a man or a beast.

One day a few years ago, a boy and his father ventured into this wilderness to hunt for deer. The boy, whose name was Jack, had just turned thirteen, and he carried his birthday present in a leather case strapped to his backpack. It was a brand-new rifle.

As the afternoon grew late, Jack and his father set up their camp in a clearing near a small creek. They built a fire and cooked their dinner. Then they sat and watched the crackling flames.

"It sure is quiet here," said Jack.

"Don't let it fool you, son. These mountains are full of creatures. Deer. Elk. Grizzlies . . ."

"I want a big buck with antlers this wide." Jack stretched his arms out to the sides as far as they could go.

"You just might get one. You've got the rifle for it. Of course you better look behind you. This is Bigfoot country."

"Bigfoot?"

His father smiled and threw another log onto the fire. For a moment, the flames disappeared beneath the wood; then the red tongues of fire reappeared, consuming the fresh fuel.

"That's right, son. From what I've heard, a grizzly's got nothing on Bigfoot. He's as tall as the trees and as wide as the mountains. The Indians used to say he was a devil who stole their animals and ate their children whole. Some folks say he's a wild man or a big ape that walks like a man. Of course other folks say he's just imagination."

"What do you say?"

Jack's father yawned and stretched. "I say it's time to go to bed. All this fresh air makes me sleepy."

"Can I stay up for a while?"

"Just for a while. Those big bucks get up early."

As his father crawled into the tent, Jack wrapped his sleeping bag around his shoulders and inched closer to the fire. The flames created a warm circle of light that disappeared into the shadows of the clearing. Beyond the clearing loomed the black forest.

Jack had a big day ahead of him, but he was too excited to turn in. He stared into the fire, imagining big bucks and other stranger creatures that walked the woods. As he daydreamed, his eyes grew heavier and heavier. Soon he was asleep.

A rustling of leaves . . . the sound of heavy footsteps. Jack opened his eyes. The fire had burned down; it was the middle of the night.

The steps grew nearer, and there was a horrible smell—worse than a skunk, worse than anything he had ever smelled before. His heart pounded in his chest. Jack glanced toward the tent where his father was sleeping.

A huge figure stood in the light of the dying flames . . .

The wooden stock of his brand-new rifle was only a few feet away, but he was afraid to move. He was afraid to breathe.

He turned back toward the fire. A huge figure stood in the light of the dying flames. Its body was covered with long hair. Its chest was broad, and its arms hung to its knees. Its face . . .

Jack gurgled in horror. He was dreaming—he had to be. It wasn't real. It had the face of an ape, with bony brow, flat nose, huge jaw, and deep black eyes. But it wasn't like any ape he had seen in a zoo. It was eight feet tall, and it stood like a man. It was Bigfoot.

Jack screamed without sound. He was too frightened for sound. Slowly, the huge creature walked around the fire. It stood directly over the boy, as tall and as massive as the giant redwoods. Then it reached down and scooped Jack up with its huge hands. Turning away from the fire, it carried the boy toward the dark woods.

"Dad!" Jack screamed. "Daaaaaad!" This time there was sound.

His father scrambled out of the tent, but all he found was a deserted fire. Jack was gone.

Deep into the woods, the creature carried the boy. Jack tried to scream, but the Bigfoot pressed his face against its broad, muscular chest. Shaggy, rank-smelling hair filled Jack's mouth. He gagged and tried to cough it out, nauseated by the sickening odor of the beast.

After what seemed like hours, the giant ape set the boy gently on the ground. Jack could hear another animal shuffling around him in the darkness. Furry hands touched his face and stroked his body. Shaking with fear and cold, Jack slumped onto the forest floor and whimpered quietly to himself.

Later, when the gray light of dawn filtered through the trees, Jack lifted his head from the ground and gazed at the beasts. A seven-foot female Bigfoot stood beside the eight-foot giant. She wasn't as heavy or as muscular as the male Bigfoot, but she was monstrous by human standards. The creatures stared at Jack as if they were waiting for him to do something. Then, very slowly, the female Bigfoot walked toward him.

"Please!" Jack begged. "Please don't hurt me!"

The Bigfoot stopped less than a yard away. Jack breathed her foul stench and looked into the black depths of her eyes. There was something very human in her gaze. Something sad, regretful . . . almost longing.

"You . . . you won't hurt me, will you?"

The Bigfoot raised her right hand and reached toward Jack's face with her long, apelike arm. Jack shrank from her approach; a low moan escaped his lips. He couldn't move. He was paralyzed by fear—and fascination.

Lightly, almost tenderly, she touched his cheek and rubbed her rough palm along the line of his jaw. She took another step forward and wrapped her long, hairy arms around him. Pulling the boy gently against her body, she cradled him as if he were a lost child. Jack felt warm and safe. For the first time since the eight-foot giant had carried him away from the fire, he was not afraid.

A shot rang out in the forest. Releasing the boy, the female Bigfoot howled in terror. "*Aaagooooummm!*" Then she turned and disappeared into the trees, followed by her mate.

Jack was alone.

"Jaaaaaaack! Jaaaaaaack!"

"Dad! Over here!"

Jack's father broke through the trees. He set his rifle against a log and held his son close. "Are you all right?" he asked. "You smell horrible!"

"It was Bigfoot!"

"Bigfoot? What are you talking about?"

As Jack told the story, his father eyed him in disbelief. "That's just a legend, son. I didn't expect you to take it seriously."

8

"It was real, Dad. I promise. Look at the tracks."

His father knelt down to examine the forest floor. There were a few broken twigs but no footprints. The ground was too hard. "I don't know, son. Maybe you had a bad dream and walked in your sleep."

"It wasn't a dream."

"C'mon, let's have some breakfast."

"Dad?"

"Yes?"

"That shot—did you hit anything?"

His father shook his head. "I was just shooting in the air."

"Good. . . . Is it okay if I don't use my rifle? I mean, can I wait until tomorrow? I just don't feel like hunting today."

Jack's father eyed him strangely. Then he smiled and shrugged. "It's your gun. Use it when you're ready."

On the way back to camp, Jack looked for signs of the Bigfoot, but there was nothing. How could two huge creatures vanish without a trace? Maybe his father was right. Maybe it really was a dream. But dreams don't smell. Do they?

When they got to their campsite, Jack examined the soft, damp ground along the creek. Huge footprints led from the edge of the forest, along the creek, and curved toward the cold remains of the fire. There was no doubt about it. He had been kidnapped by Bigfoot.

Stories of huge, hairy wild men have been told by the Indians of the Pacific Northwest for hundreds of years. The Salish Indians of British Columbia called the creature Sasquatch, which means "wild man of the woods." This name is still used in Canada today. The Huppa Indians of northern California called the creature Oh-Ma, which means "Bigfoot."

Bigfoot tracks have been found throughout the rugged mountains of northern California, Oregon, Washington, and British Columbia. These tracks are similar to barefoot human tracks, but larger, farther apart, and pressed more deeply into the ground. Most of the prints are around fourteen to eighteen inches long and five to seven inches wide. A creature with a foot of this size would be over seven feet eight inches tall and might weigh up to 800 pounds. These footprints have been found in rugged, remote areas, where it would be difficult to use a "footprint machine" to create a hoax. Some prints demonstrate special characteristics, such as deformities or dermal ridges (similar to fingerprints) that would be almost impossible to fake.

More than 2,000 people have reported seeing the Bigfoot. Most reports describe a giant, apelike creature walking on two feet like a human being. (All known apes and monkeys walk on four feet.) By combining the descriptions of many eye-witnesses, researchers have created a picture of a "typical" Bigfoot. This descrip-

tion is the basis for the two Bigfoots in this story. A few reports have described kidnapping or other aggressive behavior by the Bigfoots; however, the vast majority of reports indicate a shy creature who poses no threat to human beings.

In 1967 a man named Roger Patterson shot a short color film that appears to show a female Bigfoot walking through a clearing and into the woods. She's between six and one-half and seven feet tall, weighs about 350 pounds, and walks upright like a human being, with her arms swinging to the sides. Patterson's film has been analyzed by many experts, but no one has been able to prove whether it is real or a hoax. However, experts at Disney Studios said it would be impossible to fake such a film using a man in a costume.

Similar mysterious apelike creatures have been reported in many other areas of the world. The most famous is the Yeti, or Abominable Snowman, said to live in the Himalaya Mountains of Asia (see page 12). The Yeti seems to be somewhat smaller than the Bigfoot and sometimes travels on four feet, while the Bigfoot is always reported on two feet. Chinese scientists are investigating a large, two-footed apelike creature called the Wildman, said to live in the Shen Nong Jia Mountains of central China. Some researchers believe that the Bigfoot, the Wildman, and perhaps the Yeti, may be the descendants—or living specimens—of a prehistoric ape called Gigantopithecus.

THE YETI

KANCHE LOOKED OUT over her flock of sheep, grazing contentedly in the alpine meadow. High above the meadow, the snowy peak of Mount Everest stretched against the clear blue sky. *The top of the world,* thought Kanche. It was more than twenty miles away, but the craggy white peak looked so huge and majestic that she almost thought she could touch it.

Out of the corner of her eye, Kanche caught a flicker of movement. One of her sheep had strayed away from the flock. It was heading toward the edge of the meadow, where the rolling ground dropped off sharply into the deep valley of the Dudh Kosi River. In a single motion, Kanche ran toward the sheep, picked up a rock, and hurled it in the path of the animal. Bleating loudly, the sheep turned away and returned to the rest of the flock.

Kanche smiled proudly. Like most Sherpa children, she had been tending her family's livestock since she was very young. Her arm was strong and her aim was true. Even her brother, Tenzing, could throw no better than that. Kanche could see Tenzing at the far end of the meadow, leaning casually against a boulder as the yaks and zums grazed among the juniper bushes. Next year he would go to high school in another village. Then Kanche would watch all the animals herself.

The top of the world was bathed in brilliant sunshine, but cold shadows crept across the meadow, inching up the steep, rocky slope that rose toward the mountains. Although the meadow was green with grass, the slope was covered with eternal snow. Kanche gazed at the cold, white blanket falling gradually under the spell of darkness. Something moved in the snow, near the line between the shadows and the sunlight. Kanche rubbed her eyes and looked again. This time there was nothing. At least nothing she could see. But she felt as if something—or someone—were watching.

"Kanche! Time to go!" Tenzing broke her concentration. He was already leading the yaks and zums back toward the village.

"Wait for me!" cried Kanche. Quickly, she began to herd her sheep across the meadow. That Tenzing! He was always in such a hurry. Kanche pushed her sheep as quickly as she could. "Loh! Loh! Let's go!" She prodded them with her stick and threw rocks in the path of strays, but the sheep were slow and stupid. By the time she had them all out of the meadow and onto the road to the village, Tenzing was out of sight.

Kanche glanced back toward the rocky slope. It was covered in shadow now, but she still felt as if she were being watched. She stared through the gray twilight for signs of movement, but there was nothing. "Loh! Loh!" she called to the sheep. "Let's go!"

As she herded the animals toward the village, the darkness grew deeper and deeper. Soon even the top of the world was lost in the night. There was no moon. The only light was the soft glow of the stars.

"*Bahhhhh! Bahhhhh!*" The stillness was broken by the pitiful bleating of a sheep. Peering through the darkness, Kanche saw a huge creature on the other side of the flock. It stood upright like a man, but it was bigger and

But it wasn't a monkey. And it wasn't a man. It was the Yeti . . .

hairier than a man, with the long arms and ugly face of a monkey. Kanche watched frozen in horror as it bent over one of her sheep. It lifted the heavy animal as if it were a newborn lamb and slung it over its broad shoulders.

Kanche's horror turned to anger—it was stealing her sheep! She picked up a rock and hurled it toward the beast, hitting it squarely between the eyes.

"*Owoooooh!*" it howled in a high, hideous voice. For a moment it stared at Kanche, its red eyes glowing in the black gloom. Then it disappeared into the night, carrying the sheep.

"*Bahhhhh! Bahhhhh! Bahhhhh!*" The flock was fearful and restless. Kanche stood shaking, her teeth chattering. The night was growing cold, but it wasn't the cold that made Kanche tremble. It was the monkey-man.

"Loh! Loh!" she called. "Let's go!" Kanche tried to sound brave for the sake of the sheep. They were dumb animals; maybe they would believe her.

When Kanche reached the village, she herded the flock into the dark space beneath her family's house. The yaks and zums were already bedded down for the night. After the sheep were settled, she climbed the stairs to the living quarters. There was one large room, where her family lived, cooked, and slept. Her mother was preparing a meal of potatoes in the earthen stove. Her father, grandfather, and brother sat around the Tibetan brazier, warming themselves at the fire.

"You're late," said Tenzing.

"What's wrong, child?" asked her mother, glancing up from the cooking pot. "You look like you saw a demon!"

"I lost a sheep," said Kanche.

"What?" cried her father. "How could you lose a sheep?"

"It *was* a demon," said Kanche. "It had red eyes and the face of a monkey."

"What are you talking about?" asked her father.

"Let the girl speak," said her grandfather. "Here, child, sit by the fire."

Kanche sat beside her grandfather and told her story from the beginning, when she first saw something moving in the shadows on the snow. When she was finished, her father rose angrily and reached for the shiny rifle he had brought from Kathmandu. "A bear," he said. "I think I will teach it a lesson."

"Put the rifle away," said Kanche's grandfather. "The Sherpas do not need guns."

"What are you talking about, old man? That bear killed my sheep."

"It is not a bear. Kanche, bring me the *chang*."

Kanche crossed the great room and picked up the large jar of beerlike *chang*.

"*Chang!*" cried Kanche's father. "How is *chang* going to stop a bear?"

Kanche's grandfather rose slowly from his seat by the fire. "My son," he said, "I have told you it is not a bear. It is a Yeti. The Snowman. Come, Kanche, we have work to do."

Kanche and her grandfather walked back along the road toward the meadow. It was completely black now, and the wind howled down from the top of the world. The jar of *chang* was cold and heavy in Kanche's hands. But she was not afraid of the cold. She was afraid of the Snowman.

"Do you really think it is a Yeti?" she whispered.

Her grandfather walked briskly, shining the beam of a small flashlight on the ground ahead of them. "Of course it is a Yeti, child. I have lived in these mountains for a very long time, and I have never known a bear to have the face of a monkey or to carry a sheep and walk like a man."

"Do you think it's watching us?" asked Kanche.

The old man shrugged his shoulders. "It is possible. But we are in no danger. He has his sheep."

"But if he is full of sheep, how will he drink the *chang?*"

The old man smiled slightly, keeping his eyes on the road ahead. "He will drink. I have never known a Yeti who refused *chang*."

When they reached the place in the road where the Yeti had attacked Kanche's sheep, Kanche opened the jar of *chang* and set it on a flat rock. "Good," said her grandfather, "now we will go home and sleep."

"But what if he comes?" asked Kanche.

Her grandfather laughed and pointed the beam of the flashlight toward the village. "If he comes, he will drink. If he drinks, he will drink too much. If he drinks too much, he will sleep. If he sleeps, we will find him in the morning."

Early the next morning, before the sun rose above the mountains, Kanche and her grandfather returned to the place where they had left the *chang*. The jar was empty, and a huge shape lay beside it. The beast was over six feet tall and covered with coarse gray hair. It had the face and long, dangling arms of a monkey. But it wasn't a monkey. And it wasn't a man. It was the Yeti.

"Look, Grandfather!" cried Kanche. "There, in his forehead. You can see where I hit him with the stone."

"Your aim was true," said the old man. "I think this Yeti has a headache."

Kanche's grandfather knelt down over the sleeping beast and began to wrap a thick cord around its arms and chest. Then he wrapped another cord around its ankles. Just as he finished, the beast began to stir. "Stand back, child!" her grandfather cried. "On the other side of the road."

Kanche did as she was told. Her heart beat quickly as she watched the creature sit up slowly and look at its surroundings. It seemed confused and afraid. After a few moments it tried to stand up. When it felt the ropes, it howled like a wild man. "*Owooooooh! Owooooooh!*" The creature looked back and forth between Kanche and her grandfather, staring at them with

red, burning eyes. "*Owooooooh!*" With one great effort, it strained against the ropes and ripped them apart.

The Yeti towered above Kanche's grandfather. Kanche grabbed a rock and took careful aim at the beast. When the Yeti saw the rock in Kanche's hand, it howled in terror and ran toward the meadow. It fled like a wild man across the rolling ground and scrambled up the rocky slope, disappearing into the eternal snow.

Kanche's grandfather stood beside the empty jar of *chang*, a broken piece of rope in his bony hands, gazing sadly toward the slope. "They will never believe us," he said.

Kanche dropped the rock. Then she crossed the road and put her arms around the old man. "That's all right, Grandfather. We know the truth."

"Yes"—he nodded—"and so does that Yeti." Slowly his old wrinkled face broke into a broad grin. "I don't think we'll be losing any more sheep."

———

Stories of mysterious wild men have been told by the people of the Himalayas for hundreds of years—they are especially common among the Sherpas, a tribe of hardy, cheerful people who live beneath Mount Everest in Nepal. Many ideas in this story, including the Yeti's fondness for chang, are based on Sherpa folktales.

The word Yeti is an English version of yeh-teh, a Nepalese word that means "snowman." The term Abominable Snowman comes from the Tibetan name for the creature, Metoh-Kangmi, which means "filthy or disgusting snowman."

Since the early nineteenth century, British diplomats, military officers, and explorers have reported seeing strange creatures or footprints in the Himalayas. However, it was not until 1951 that the Yeti became famous in the Western world. A British mountain climber named Eric Shipton discovered a strange set of footprints on the Menlung Glacier at an elevation of 18,000 feet. On the same day, he discovered another print that was thirteen inches long and eight inches wide with clearly defined toes. Shipton's photographs of the footprints were published throughout the world.

During the last forty years, scientific and mountaineering expeditions have continued to encounter strange footprints in the snows of the Himalayas. In 1970, a British mountain climber named Don Whillans photographed supposed Yeti tracks at an elevation of 13,000 feet. That night—in bright moonlight—Whillans observed an apelike creature running on four legs across a hillside. In 1986, German mountaineer Reinhold Messner claimed to see a Yeti at a range of thirty feet. The same year, British physicist Anthony Wooldridge photographed a set of footprints and a "creature" that some experts believed to be a Yeti. Wooldridge later proved that the "creature" was a rock, but the footprints remain a mystery.

At first, it was believed that the Yeti lived in a very small area of the Himalayas. However, Yeti-like creatures have also been sighted in China and the Soviet Union. The Yeti seems to be smaller than the Bigfoot, and it apparently walks on four legs as well as on two legs. Some researchers believe that the Yeti and the Bigfoot are related; others think they may be two different creatures.

THE ALMAS

ANNA STOOD IN the doorway and looked back at her mother. "I'm going."

"Hmm. That's nice, dear."

Anna's mother was bent over the old wooden desk, studying her notebooks as if they were the most important things in the world. She called it scientific research. Anna called it boring.

"I said, I'm going, Mother."

"Yes, dear. I heard you. Be home for supper."

Anna whirled in the doorway and stomped down the stone path toward the road. What a horrible vacation! She was stuck in the mountains with nothing to do while her friends went to parties in Moscow. And all because her mother wanted to chase some silly wild man called an Almas. Why, even her mother's friends at the academy thought she was crazy.

Anna stopped at the end of the path and looked up the road toward the village. It was an easy walk—less than a kilometer. But what was the point? There was nothing to do in the village anyway. The children stared at her as if she were from another world, just because she wore city clothes. Why, they didn't even speak Russian!

She decided to walk away from the village, toward the thick forest that covered the mountainside. It was beautiful in the woods—cool and dark and secret. She had brought some bread and a piece of chicken in her knapsack. Perhaps she would have a picnic.

After three-quarters of an hour, Anna came to a rushing stream that ran into the heart of the woods. She knelt down and took a long drink of the cool water. Leaving the road, she followed the stream through the towering green trees. She hopped from rock to rock over the water, pretending she was a creature of the forest.

After a while, the forest opened onto a small clearing full of tall golden sunflowers. Anna was delighted. Such big, beautiful flowers! It was the perfect place for a picnic. She set her knapsack on a patch of grass and took out the bread and chicken. As she chewed her food, she looked around at the tall stems of the sunflowers. It was like being in a tiny forest all her own. A forest of flowers!

Something moved beyond the flowers. A shape—an animal! Anna held her breath in fear. What could it be? A bear? A wolf? No—something human. A human face staring at her through the tall green stems of the sunflowers. It was a girl!

"Hello," said Anna cautiously. "Do you speak Russian?"

The girl made a strange, whimpering sound. It was not like any language Anna had ever heard. *These mountain people!*

"My name is Anna. What's your name?"

The girl continued to stare through the green stems. *She certainly is ugly,* thought Anna. Her forehead stuck out above her eyebrows, and her nose was pressed back against her face. Her hair was long and stringy. And she hardly had any chin at all.

"Would you like some bread? Or a bite of chicken?" Anna held the food toward the strange girl.

Then she stood up and disappeared into the sunflowers.

The girl emerged from her hiding place and snatched the chicken out of Anna's hand. She took a huge bite and chewed loudly, the muscles of her jaws protruding from the sides of her face. Anna could hear the cracking of small chicken bones.

Anna was so surprised by the sudden movement and the fierce chewing that it took her a moment to realize the girl was naked. From a distance, the red hair covering her thick, muscular body almost looked like clothing. Although the strange girl was smaller than Anna, she looked strong enough to tear her to pieces. She was almost like an animal. But she wasn't an animal. Was she?

When the girl had finished the chicken, Anna handed her the piece of bread. "Poor thing, you must be starving!"

The strange girl ate the bread and held out her hand for more. Her upturned palm was hairless and wrinkled and dark. Her face was dark, too—as if she had spent her life in the sun.

"I'm sorry," said Anna. "I don't have any more food."

The girl continued to hold her wrinkled palm out toward Anna. "I'm sorry," Anna repeated.

Baring huge white teeth, the strange girl snarled like a wild dog.

Anna jumped to her feet and ran through the sunflowers toward the edge of the forest. When she reached the trees, she remembered her knapsack. It was expensive; her mother had bought it at one of the best stores in Moscow. Cautiously, Anna worked her way back through the tall flowers. The strange girl was holding the knapsack and whimpering with that pitiful sound.

"It's empty," said Anna. "But if you give it to me, I will fill it with food and come back tomorrow." She approached the girl hesitantly and took the knapsack from her wrinkled hands. "Tomorrow," she repeated. "I will see you tomorrow."

The next day Anna packed chicken, sausage, bread, and cheese and returned to the forest. The strange girl was waiting in the sunflowers, just where Anna had left her. Anna sat beside her and opened the knapsack, handing her the food piece by piece. When it was gone, the girl held out her wrinkled palm for more. This time there was no snarl.

"Tomorrow," said Anna.

With a tiny whimper, the girl brought her hand back toward her body. Then she stood up and disappeared into the sunflowers. Her light, quick movements caught Anna by surprise. As quickly as she had disappeared, the girl returned to the patch of grass. Once again she extended her wrinkled palm. There were three small red berries in the center of her hand.

Anna took the berries and held them in the sunlight. They looked harmless enough. She took a small bite and then popped them all in her mouth. They were delicious.

"Thank you," she said.

The strange girl stretched her thick lips back over her huge white teeth. It was almost like a smile.

"You must have a name," said Anna. "Everyone has a name. I know—I'll call you Sunflower. Tomorrow, Sunflower. I will see you again tomorrow."

And so it went throughout the summer. Each day Anna returned to the forest, bringing food for Sunflower. And each day Sunflower brought small gifts of her own—acorns, berries, leaves. Once she even brought a dead field mouse. It was disgusting, but Anna tried to be polite. After all, they were friends.

All too soon the time came for Anna and her mother to return to Moscow. As they packed their belongings, Anna worried about Sunflower. How would she survive? Would she live on mice and acorns?

"Are you ready, Anna?"

"Yes, Mother."

"Good. Tell me, dear, did you enjoy your vacation?"

"Oh yes, Mother, it was wonderful!"

"I'm so glad. I was afraid you would be lonely here."

"Oh, not at all. The forest is so beautiful." For a moment, Anna considered telling her mother about Sunflower. Perhaps they could take her with them to Moscow. But no, that would never do. Sunflower didn't belong in Moscow. She belonged in the sunflower forest.

"Tell me, Mother, did you enjoy *your* vacation?"

Anna's mother laughed. "Why yes, dear. I did. Of course, these mountain people can be difficult with strangers, but I think I have enough eyewitness reports to construct a picture of the Almas. I've even done a preliminary sketch. Would you like to see it?"

"Yes, please."

Anna's mother opened her briefcase and removed a sheet of rough sketching paper. Anna took the paper from her outstretched hand and glanced at the image. Then she looked again. And again. It was just a quick sketch in pencil, but it was almost a perfect likeness. The stringy hair. The protruding forehead. The flattened nose. The receding chin. Even the short red body hair. It was Sunflower. It was her friend—the Almas.

———————

Strange humanlike creatures have been observed in the mountains of Mongolia, China, and the Soviet Union for many hundreds of years. The native people of these regions call the creatures by many different names. However, most researchers use the Mongolian term, Almas. No one knows exactly what it means, but it might be translated as "wild man."

During the first half of the twentieth century, a number of Russian and Mongolian scientists studied the Almas in Mongolia. Some of their research was lost; some was hidden by the government because it feared embarrassment in the scientific world. In 1958 the Soviet Academy of Sciences established the "Snowman Commission" to study reports of humanlike creatures living in the high mountains. An expedition to the rugged Pamir Mountains of the south-central Soviet Union found interesting stories but no definite proof.

A scientist who took part in the Pamir expedition, Dr. Marie-Jeanne Koffmann, then began studying the Almas in the Caucasus Mountains of the southwestern Soviet Union. Unlike most regions where the Almas has been spotted, the Caucasus has a large human population. By 1966 Dr. Koffmann had gathered over 300 eyewitness reports. From these reports, she was able to describe a "typical" Almas. Dr. Koffmann's description, along with other details from her reports, forms the basis of this story.

Early researchers considered the Almas and the Yeti to be different names for the same creature. They called it the wild man, the Missing Link, or the Abominable Snowman. It now seems that there are at least two very different species of

"Snowman." The Yeti (and its cousin the Bigfoot) is usually described as a huge apelike creature. The Almas is usually described as a smaller and more primitive form of human being.

Some scientists believe that the Almas is a surviving Neanderthal man. According to this theory, as modern man developed and used more land, Neanderthal man was pushed higher and higher into the mountains. It is interesting that the main areas of Almas sightings are near places where Neanderthal tools and skeletons have been found. Now that communication is growing between the Soviet Union and the United States, perhaps someday soon we will know the true story of the Almas.

THE LOCH NESS MONSTER

ROBBIE MACGREGOR held his binoculars and studied the dark, churning waters of Loch Ness. About 500 yards from the shore, three cormorants bobbed up and down in the choppy waves. A casual observer might have thought they were three humps of the monster, but Robbie could see their separate bodies and the outline of their wings. His binoculars were powerful, and besides, he was no casual observer. He was an investigator.

Robbie passed over the birds and scanned the width of the loch toward Urquhart Castle, looming on the opposite shore. It was the middle of July, but a cold wind was blowing in from the North Sea. Nothing but waves and more waves. It was a bad day for Nessie. Most of the sightings took place on clear, warm summer days when the water was smooth as glass. Today, the loch looked more like a mixing bowl.

He continued scanning the waves toward the northeast. An object floated just above the waterline, but it was too big for Nessie. Probably a trawler. He angled the glasses upward and studied the sky. Storm clouds were gathering over Inverness.

"If I had any sense, I'd go home," he mumbled.

Robbie let the binoculars dangle while he checked his camera. It was equipped with a telephoto lens and high-speed film. If Nessie showed, he wanted a good, clear shot of her. That was the only way to really prove she exists—once and for all. He adjusted the focus ring on the lens. Then he raised his binoculars and scanned the loch again.

Like most Highlanders, Robbie had heard stories of Nessie for as long as he could remember. He had spent hours looking into the deep, murky waters of Loch Ness, waiting patiently for the creature to appear. But he had never seen her. Finally, he had convinced his parents to let him camp out on the beach. After all, he was sixteen now, and the real investigators spent days, even weeks, camped along the shore.

Robbie glanced again at the clouds over Inverness. Of course the real investigators had nice dry vans or trailers to protect them from the weather. He looked back across the narrow, rocky beach to his pup tent; it was better than nothing. And the cliffs would provide some protection. The main thing was to keep the camera dry. He reached into the pocket of his mackintosh, pulled out a plastic bag, and slipped it over the long telephoto lens.

In the early evening, it began to drizzle. Robbie stood on the rocky shore, scanning the loch through the fine, gray rain. The light was still good. But as the rain grew harder, the sky darkened, and the churning waters of the loch turned black as pitch.

"Achhh! I couldn't tell Nessie from a log in this weather." With a sigh of disappointment, Robbie crossed the beach and crawled into his tent.

The heart of the storm arrived around midnight. The rain pounded on the sides of the tent, and the wind howled through the flaps. Robbie lay awake, listening to the sounds of the storm and thinking of the deep black waters of the loch. "Where are you, Nessie?" he asked aloud. "Do you like the rain?"

A black hump emerged from the foam. . . . It was Nessie!

Sometime in the early morning, Robbie fell into a dreamless sleep. He was awakened by the sound of a cormorant, cawing loudly as it hunted for fish. Robbie opened his eyes slowly and stared at the roof of the tent. Except for the noisy bird, everything was quiet. Quiet! The rain was over!

He crawled from the tent and gazed out over the loch. The rising sun was shining on the hills near Urquhart Castle. The wind and clouds were gone. The water was smooth as glass.

Robbie caught a sudden flash of movement a hundred yards from the shore. The water began to bubble and boil with thick foam. Robbie ran across the beach to the edge of the loch. A black hump emerged from the foam. It looked like an overturned boat. But it wasn't a boat. It was Nessie!

He reached down for his binoculars. "Achhh!" They were still in the tent. The camera, too.

Out in the water, the hump was growing and growing. It was huge! Now a smaller hump appeared in front of the big one; it was growing, too, curving upward. No, it wasn't a hump at all. It was her neck. And her head. Nessie was looking at him!

Robbie gazed in wonder at the huge hump, the long neck, the tiny head—all black and glistening in the rising sun. "Hello, Nessie," he whispered. "Stay right where you are."

Very slowly he began to back up over the narrow beach, keeping Nessie in his sight. "One picture," he pleaded. "Just one good picture." He was almost at the tent now, and she was still posing motionless in the water. The camera was in the plastic bag, tucked in his pack in the back of the tent. It would take ten seconds—maybe less. He knelt down on the rocks. Then he scrambled into the tent, grabbed the camera, and scrambled back onto the beach. He stared at the loch in disbelief. Nessie was gone.

"Achhh!" Robbie moaned. He walked back down to the shore and examined the surface of the loch. A circle of waves remained where Nessie had

disappeared. The waves spread outward and outward, finally lapping at the rocks beneath his feet.

For a long time, Robbie scanned the loch for signs of Nessie. But there was nothing. He had seen her. And she was gone—back to her home in the cold, deep water.

Finally, he tore down his tent and packed away his binoculars and his camera with the telephoto lens. The investigation was over—at least for now.

Before he left, Robbie stood one last time on the rocky shore and looked out over the dark, waveless loch. A slight smile crept over his face. "Good-bye, Nessie," he said. "I'll see you again."

Loch Ness is a deep, dark lake in the Highlands of Scotland. For centuries, the people who live near the loch have told stories of a strange beast living in the murky waters. However, 1933 was the year that made Nessie famous. Over ninety people claimed to have seen the monster that year, and many of these stories were published in newspapers throughout the world. The sightings increased in 1934, with over 130 reports. A new road was built along the loch during these years, bringing more people to the area and allowing a better view of the water. Also, it's believed the dynamite used in building the road may have brought Nessie to the surface.

Today, over 4,000 people have claimed to have seen the Loch Ness Monster. Some of these reports were hoaxes, and others were sightings of normal objects or animals mistaken in the distance. But there still remain hundreds of sightings by reliable witnesses.

The general picture of Nessie from these reports is of a dark creature twenty to forty feet long, with at least one hump rising above the water, a long, thin neck, and a small head. Although most sightings take place in the water, a few people say they have seen Nessie on the land.

There have been many photographs of the creature, but none are clear enough to provide absolute proof that it exists. A film taken by Tim Dinsdale in 1960 is one of the strongest pieces of evidence. It shows an object moving through the water without the kind of waves that would be created by a boat. The film was analyzed by British military intelligence experts in 1966. They concluded that it was probably an animal at least six feet wide, five feet high, and twelve to sixteen feet long.

Since the mid-1960s, investigators have used sophisticated technology to look for Nessie. In 1968 sonar readings by scientists from the University of Birmingham indicated that there was a group of large animals in the loch, diving to great depths at surprising speeds. An underwater photograph taken in 1972 appears to show a large flipper; another photograph taken in 1975 seems to show the outline of a long-necked beast with a large body and two fins. Divers and mini-submarines have also searched for Nessie, but they have been hampered by the poor visibility in the murky water.

Early researchers imagined Nessie to be a single creature that had wandered into Loch Ness from the sea. It is now clear that, if Nessie exists, there must be a whole population of large, unknown animals living and breeding in Loch Ness. The question is, what are they? Researchers have considered different types of creatures: 1) a long-necked aquatic mammal related to a seal or manatee; 2) a long, thin whale similar to the zeuglodon, thought to have become extinct 25 million years ago; 3) an aquatic reptile similar to the plesiosaur, thought to have become extinct 65 million years ago; 4) an amphibian similar to a giant salamander or newt; 5) a giant eel; or 6) an invertebrate similar to a giant worm or sea slug.

Nessie is only one of many strange creatures that have been reported living in cold, deep lakes in the Northern Hemisphere. Other famous lake monsters include Ogapogo, in Lake Okanagan, located in British Columbia, and Champie, in Lake Champlain, located in upper New York State. Monsters have been reported in other Scottish lakes, as well as in Ireland, Sweden, and the Soviet Union. These creatures may all be the same type of animal, but the evidence suggests that there may be more than one kind of unknown animal living in the cold lakes of the north.

THE LUSCA

ENJAMIN PUSHED OFF from the rocky shore and sculled with one of the long wooden oars. As he disturbed the crystal-clear water, a school of tiny, iridescent fish scattered into a maze of pink coral. Benjamin smiled. *Grow big,* he thought. *Perhaps we will meet again.*

When the dinghy was free of the underwater rocks, Benjamin set the oars in place and pulled away from the island. In the bow, his older brother, Caleb, gazed out over the clear blue water. "Pull, Benjamin," said Caleb. "The fish are waiting."

"I'm pulling," said Benjamin. It was early morning, but the sun was already hot, and he could feel salty sweat dripping into his eyes.

"Do you want me to do it?" asked Caleb.

"No," said Benjamin, straining hard against the long wooden oars. "I can do it myself."

After an hour of hard pulling, they were beyond the reef and into the Tongue of the Ocean, the deep blue water that stretches to the east of Andros Island in the Bahamas. Caleb stood in the bow of the dinghy and surveyed the surface with the practiced eye of an expert. Finally, he pointed to an indigo-blue patch of water. "There," he said. "I can feel the fish."

Like a vicious whip, a giant tentacle broke the surface . . .

Benjamin rowed quickly toward the dark blue patch. Sometimes it was difficult to be Caleb's brother, but to fish with him was an honor. When Caleb could feel the fish, the catch would be big.

"All right," said Caleb. "Now scull gently while I let out the line."

Benjamin worked the oars easily through the water, trying to keep the boat steady as Caleb let the huge coil of line run through his hands. When the line was out, Caleb began to bring it up, slowly and steadily. Benjamin smiled in admiration of his brother's strong, sure movements. The tourists used big powerboats and thick poles with metal reels, but Caleb needed nothing but a dinghy and a handline. That, and a good partner to keep the boat steady.

When the line was halfway into the boat, Caleb's face grew strained; he began to breathe heavily.

"What's wrong?" asked Benjamin.

"The line's stuck. It must be caught on the bottom."

"What should I do?"

"Row in a circle—very slowly."

Benjamin did as he was told. In the bow of the dinghy, Caleb strained on the handline, trying to loosen it from the bottom. Sweat ran down his face, and the muscles in his arms seemed ready to explode. Finally, with one great effort, the line began to move.

"Is it loose?" asked Benjamin.

"It's off the bottom," said Caleb, still straining on the handline. "But it's caught on something . . . very . . . heavy."

"Maybe it's a big fish."

"No, the big fish fight . . . or move. This is just hanging on the line."

"Maybe it's treasure!"

Caleb smiled slightly as he continued to pull the handline into the dinghy. "We'll know . . . soon enough."

When most of the line was coiled in the bow, Caleb leaned over slightly and looked down.

"What is it?" asked Benjamin.

Caleb continued to stare into the water, pulling on the handline. Suddenly his face contorted in horror. "No!"

Like a vicious whip, a giant tentacle broke the surface and wrapped around Caleb's body. Another tentacle exploded on the side of the boat and circled the dinghy as if it were a toy. "Help!" cried Caleb. "The Lusca!"

Benjamin grabbed a wooden oar and pounded the rubbery mass of flesh that stretched across the dinghy separating him from Caleb. The tentacle was as thick as a man's body; the huge suckers held the boat like a powerful adhesive. The Lusca was pulling the dinghy downward into the Tongue of the Ocean. Then suddenly the giant arm arched high in the air and disappeared into the sea. Benjamin looked desperately toward the bow of the dinghy. Caleb was gone!

Rushing to the front of the boat, Benjamin peered down into the water. The Lusca writhed directly below him—a huge bulbous head and eight grotesque arms that stretched as far as he could see—one arm still coiled tightly around Caleb.

Caleb was struggling fiercely. But he couldn't hold out for long underwater.

Benjamin grabbed a fish knife and dove into the water, swimming down toward Caleb. After what seemed like hours, he reached his brother. Benjamin hacked at the rubbery tentacle—it was useless. The creature's flesh was hard and thick; the giant suckers held Caleb imprisoned in their deadly grasp.

Lungs ready to burst, Benjamin swam toward the monstrous head. Now he was face to face with the Lusca. Its eyes were like great saucers, looking back at him with a strange, horrible intelligence. Benjamin tightened his

grip on the fish knife and drove the blade deep into the eye of the Lusca.

The sea was filled with inky blackness. Benjamin fought through the dark water toward Caleb, groping desperately for his brother's body. His lungs were burning, and his head was spinning, but that didn't matter. It was Caleb that mattered. He had to find Caleb.

He brushed against something in the darkness. Soft flesh. Human flesh. Caleb—floating freely in the inky water. The Lusca was gone.

Breaking the surface, Benjamin gasped for air, filling his lungs again and again. Then he boosted Caleb into the dinghy and struggled in after him. He laid his palms against his brother's chest and pushed. Water spurted out of Caleb's lungs, and Benjamin blew breath back into his body. Again and again, Benjamin pressed and blew, pressed and blew, until Caleb began to breathe on his own. After a few shallow breaths, Caleb's eyes fluttered open. He was alive.

"How do you feel?" asked Benjamin.

Caleb smiled weakly. "Thank you," he said.

"Is anything broken?"

"I don't think so. But my back hurts."

"Let me see." Carefully Benjamin rolled his brother over. Caleb yelped with pain. In the center of his back was a large round wound where the skin had been torn away, exposing the bloody red tissue underneath. It was a perfect circle—the size of a sucker on the monster's arm. It was the mark of the Lusca.

———

Sailors have told stories of sea monsters for as long as man has sailed the sea. One of the most famous monsters was the Kraken, a huge, many-armed creature reported by Norwegian sailors in the north Atlantic. For hundreds of years, most people considered the Kraken to be a fantasy animal. Then, in the 1870s, animals very similar to the Kraken began to wash up on the beaches of Newfoundland—across the Atlantic from Norway. Upon examining these creatures, scientists discovered that they were giant squid. The largest known specimen of giant squid is around sixty feet long, but some experts believe there may be specimens twice that size.

Although the giant squid probably explains the tales of the Kraken, the Lusca is another story. The Lusca is a many-armed monster—half octopus, half dragon—reported by natives of Andros Island in the Bahamas. It is said to live in inland lakes and water-filled holes, as well as in the depths of the ocean. Just as most scientists once believed that the Kraken was a myth, many believe that the Lusca is a creature of fantasy. Others think the Lusca is a giant squid. Some scientists and fishermen, however, believe that the Lusca is really a giant octopus.

Unlike the giant squid, the giant octopus has not yet been officially accepted by the scientific world. But there is strong evidence that the giant octopus does exist and that it may be even larger than the giant squid—perhaps as long as 200 feet from tentacle tip to tentacle tip! It's difficult to estimate the weight of such a creature, but it would certainly weigh many tons. (The largest known octopus measures about twenty feet from tip to tip and weighs around 125 pounds.)

The strongest evidence for the existence of the giant octopus is a carcass that washed up on the beach of St. Augustine, Florida, in 1896. Although the carcass was partially decayed, those who examined it believed that it was the remains of a huge octopus. Pieces of arms were found buried in the sand nearby; the longest measured over thirty-two feet. Based on the size of the carcass and the partial arms, the octopus would have had arms seventy-five to one hundred feet long, thus measuring between 150 and 200 feet from tip to tip. The carcass alone—without the arms—was estimated to weigh six tons.

In 1897 Professor A. E. Verrill, a highly respected expert on cephalopods—animals like the octopus and squid—agreed that the Florida sea monster was probably an octopus. After studying photographs and tissue samples, Dr. Verrill gave it the scientific name Octopus giganteus, which means "giant octopus." However, Dr. Verrill later changed his mind, without ever examining the carcass. Fortunately, a sample of the carcass was preserved at the Smithsonian Institution. Over seventy years later, a team of scientists discovered this sample and tested it using modern laboratory techniques. These tests indicate that the Florida sea monster was more similar to the octopus than to any other known animal.

The giant squid and giant octopus may explain many-armed sea monsters like the Kraken and the Lusca. However, most reports of sea monsters describe long necks or snakelike bodies. These are often called sea serpents. The zoologist Bernard Heuvelmans has studied almost 600 reports of sea serpents over the centuries. He believes these reports may be based on at least seven different unknown animals. Science has solved the mystery of the Kraken by discovering the giant squid, and the mystery of the Lusca may be solved with the discovery of the giant octopus. Perhaps some day the mystery of the sea serpents may be solved as well.

THE MOKELE-MBEMBE

DAHKA STALKED THROUGH the dark forest in the way of the great Pygmy hunters. His eyes missed nothing; his ears were tuned to the slightest sound. For years he had watched his father and the other men of the band. Now it was his turn to bring home the evening meal.

Dahka turned toward a rustling in the rotting leaves and watched a python slither across the muddy floor of the forest. His heart beat quickly with excitement. He had been hunting since early morning, and this was the biggest animal he had seen. *It is a good python,* he thought. *It will make many meals.*

The boy reached into his quiver and withdrew a poisoned arrow. In one smooth motion, he placed the arrow into his crossbow, pulled back on the string, and aimed at the vulnerable spot between the eyes of the snake. Before he could release the arrow, a monkey screeched loudly in the trees, warning the other monkeys that the deadly python was approaching.

"Hoo hoo hoo hoo! Hoo hoo hoo hoo!"

For a moment, Dahka took his eyes off the snake and turned toward the noisy monkey. When he looked back at the ground, the python had disappeared into the thick green vegetation.

"Stupid monkey," he muttered angrily. "Come down where I can see you, and I'll take *you* home for supper."

Dahka continued onward, pushing and hacking his way through the thick vegetation. Although it was the dry season, his feet sank into the muddy ooze. Occasionally, he would step into a puddle and sink up to his knees. The Likouala swamps were not an easy place to walk. But they made an excellent place to hunt.

In the early afternoon, Dahka broke through the edge of the swampy forest and stood on the shore of Lake Telle. After the dense forest, the broad, flat lake seemed enormous. Dahka could barely see the opposite shore.

Holding his crossbow above his head, Dahka waded out into the dark water. The lake was very shallow, and even a Pygmy could walk near the shore. It was easier than walking through the forest, and there were plenty of crocodiles and turtles to hunt.

Near the shore, perhaps a kilometer away, Dahka noticed a disturbance in the smooth surface of the lake. Something was emerging from the water. It looked like a snake, but a snake cannot stand up straight in the water. Dahka gazed across the surface. *What is it?* he wondered. *It's not a fish or a crocodile, and it's too big to be a turtle. Maybe it's the trunk of an elephant!* If he killed an elephant, he would be a great hunter. The whole band would have a feast!

Dahka waded toward the animal, quickly yet silently. He passed crocodiles and turtles swimming in the shallow water, but he was not interested in them. *What hunter would want a turtle if he could have an elephant?*

As Dahka drew closer, the elephant's trunk looked stranger and stranger.

Dahka stared in horror as a huge dark shape emerged from the molibo.

There seemed to be a huge eye and a small head at the end, but he was still too far away to see clearly. Perhaps it was just the angle. Or a trick of the light. He would know soon enough.

When Dahka was within a few hundred meters of the animal, the trunk began to move toward a muddy stream—a *molibo*—flowing into the lake. Dahka waded desperately toward the mouth of the stream. He had to catch the elephant before it disappeared into the forest. He reached the mouth and began to wade upstream through the murky water of the molibo. Soon he was surrounded by the dark forest. The water was up to his chest, and thick patches of floating grass grabbed his arms like water snakes.

Panting with exhaustion, Dahka stopped and gazed up the molibo into the dense forest. There was no sign of the elephant. If it had left the water, he would have heard it and seen tracks on the shore. No, it was still in the molibo. *But where is it?* he wondered. *Elephants do not disappear.*

Suddenly, the water exploded around him. Dahka stared in horror as a huge dark shape emerged from the molibo. It grew larger and larger until it was bigger than an elephant—bigger than two elephants or three elephants! Its massive body glistened in the sun. Its powerful tail was like a great tree floating on the surface of the molibo. It had a neck like a python, a head like a giant turtle, and cold crocodile eyes that stared down at Dahka as if he were nothing more than a piece of floating grass.

No, it was not an elephant. It was the monster of the swamps. Mokele-Mbembe.

Dahka stared wide-eyed at the huge beast towering above him and gripped his crossbow tightly in his hands. His heart was beating louder than a thousand drums, but his hunter's instinct took control. He reached for a poisoned arrow, set it into the crossbow, and pulled back on the string.

Like a flash of lightning, Mokele-Mbembe's powerful tail whipped across the water and smashed Dahka into the molibo. The boy struggled

45

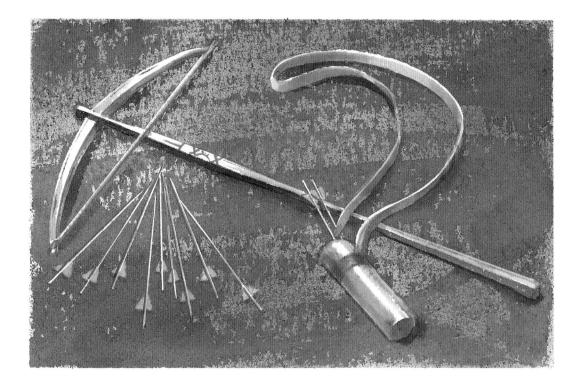

in the floating grass, gasping for breath as he tried to regain his footing. His crossbow was gone. He was at the mercy of the monster.

Back on his feet, Dahka found himself staring directly into the cold eyes of Mokele-Mbembe. For a moment, the beast seemed to contemplate whether the boy might make a good meal. Then the monster turned its heavy body and waded toward the shore. Dahka watched as Mokele-Mbembe stopped to eat the molombo fruit that grew along the edge of the stream. When it had eaten its fill, the great beast stepped out of the water and smashed its way through the trees.

After Mokele-Mbembe was gone, Dahka searched for his crossbow in the muddy bottom of the molibo. When he found it, he waded across the stream and climbed onto the bank. He breathed deeply and tried to steady his heart.

The path of the monster was like an open road through the swamps—

wide enough for two elephants to walk side by side. Dahka followed the path for a few steps; then he walked into the darkness of the forest. It was late, and he was empty-handed. Perhaps he would find that python. If not, maybe the monkey.

―――――――――

Huge monsters that look like dinosaurs have been reported by the natives of tropical Africa for at least 200 years. The description of these creatures is similar to that of a sauropod, a plant-eating dinosaur with a massive body, powerful tail, long neck, and small head. The sauropods were the largest animals ever to live on land. One type of sauropod, Diplodocus, was eighty-two feet long; another type, Brachiosaurus, weighed fifty tons. However, the sauropods reported from Africa are probably much smaller than these extremes.

The modern search for living sauropods began in the late 1970s. A scientist named James Powell showed pictures of various animals to the native people of Gabon, located along the equator in central Africa. When he showed them a picture of a sauropod, they identified it as "N'yamala" and said that it lived in remote jungle lakes. Powell reported his findings to another scientist named Roy Mackal, and together they planned an expedition to search for the N'yamala.

After studying the historical reports, Powell and Mackal concluded that the N'yamala was the same animal as the Mokele-Mbembe, a sauropodlike creature described by the people of the Congo, located east of Gabon. The scientists also concluded that the best place to look for Mokele-Mbembe would be the Likouala swamps in the northeastern part of the Congo. In 1980, Powell and Mackal went to the Likouala region and interviewed the Pygmies and Bantus who live near the swamps. The next year, Mackal returned with a second expedition. Although these expeditions found no definite proof, they obtained many additional reports from native people.

At the same time that the second Mackal expedition was exploring the rivers of the Likouala region, another American expedition, led by an engineer named Herman Regusters, reached Lake Telle in the heart of the swamps. Regusters claimed to have photographed Mokele-Mbembe in the lake. However, the photographs were not clear, and other information provided by Regusters was confusing.

In 1983 a new expedition was led by a Congolese zoologist, Marcellin Agnagna. Agnagna claimed to have seen Mokele-Mbembe in Lake Telle. As a trained zoologist, Agnagna was familiar with the animals that live in the Likouala swamps, and he was unlikely to mistake one animal for another. He described Mokele-Mbembe as a reptile approximately sixteen feet long above the water, with a broad black back, a long neck, a small head, and oval crocodilian eyes. He drew a sketch that looks very similar to a sauropod.

Since 1983 there have been at least three additional expeditions to the Likouala swamps, one British group and two Japanese groups. None of these expeditions has seen Mokele-Mbembe. The second Japanese group reported that the creature probably does not actually live in Lake Telle, but rather in the molibos, small jungle streams that flow into the lake.

Is there a living dinosaur in the swamps of the Congo? To the native people, Mokele-Mbembe is as real as the elephant or the monkey. Herman Regusters and Marcellin Agnagna claim to have seen it. Scientists like Roy Mackal and James Powell think it is very possible. The tropical swamps of central Africa were never covered with ice during the Ice Ages, and they have changed relatively little since the days of the dinosaurs, over 65 million years ago. Mokele-Mbembe may be waiting for the next expedition.

THE KONGAMATO

THE JIUNDU RIVER snaked its way through the thick green swamp. As the hunting party approached the bank, Mbula held up his hand, and the porters came to a stop. The white hunter wiped the sweat from his forehead and turned toward the African boy.

"What's wrong?" asked the hunter.

"The river," said Mbula.

"I can see the blasted river," said the hunter. "Is it deep?"

"No, sir," said Mbula. "Very shallow."

"Well, let's cross it."

Mbula glanced politely away from the older man. "Soon, sir. Very soon."

Reaching into his bag, Mbula removed the mulendi root and the cup made of bark. Then, squatting on the soft, swampy ground, he began to cut the root into strips with his sharp knife.

"What in blazes are you doing?" asked the hunter.

"*Muchi wa Kongamato*," said Mbula quietly.

"Speak English, boy."

"It is a protection."

"A protection? Against what?"

49

Out of the sky, a huge red monster swooped toward the hunter . . .

Mbula's voice dropped to a whisper: "Kongamato."

"What in blazes is Kongamato?"

"Please, sir," Mbula begged. "It is better that we do not speak of it."

When the mulendi root had been cut into narrow strips, Mbula took a piece of vine from his bag and tied half of the strips into a small bundle. Then he set the remaining strips on a flat rock and began to grind them with the back of his knife. The white hunter stood above him impatiently, staring angrily at the river and wiping the sweat from his forehead. Forming a small circle around them, the porters watched in deadly seriousness.

"This is ridiculous," said the hunter finally. "I'm not going to stand and wait for this blasted native witchcraft. If you're afraid of Kongawhatcha-callit, that's fine. I'm crossing the river." Breaking through the circle, the hunter headed for the muddy Jiundu.

"Please, sir," cried Mbula. "Wait for protection!" Acting quickly, the boy scooped the powdered root into the cup. Then he poured a bit of water from his canteen onto the powder until it became a thin, watery paste. When the mixture was ready, he rose to his feet and ran after the white hunter. "Please, sir! Wait!"

The hunter was already halfway into the river, up to his waist in the muddy water, holding his rifle high above his head. Just as Mbula reached the bank, a great wind whipped the water and shook the tops of the trees.

Out of the sky, a huge red monster swooped toward the white hunter. Its wings were half as wide as the river. Knife-sharp teeth flashed in its long, ugly beak, and razorlike claws curled from its feet and hands. It was a bird and a lizard and a bat in one horrible nightmare. It was the Kongamato.

Running toward the hunter, Mbula dipped his bundle of root strips into the cup and sprinkled the paste onto the surface of the water. "*Muchi wa Kongamato*," he chanted. "*Muchi wa Kongamato*."

Out in the water, the hunter turned toward the flying monster and raised

his rifle. He was too late. The Kongamato swooped down and knocked the gun from his hands as if it were a twig. The hunter tumbled into the muddy water of the Jiundu, his arms and legs flailing like a madman's.

A moment later, Mbula reached the center of the river and pulled the hunter to the surface. He had swallowed water, but there were no cuts or bruises. Slinging the man's arm over his shoulder, the boy helped him back to the shore. He made him comfortable on the swampy ground and poured cool, clean water over his face. The hunter was still breathing heavily, and his eyes were glazed with terror. But he would recover.

"You are very brave, sir," said Mbula soothingly. "Few white men have seen the swamp of the Jiundu. But you are foolish, too. Next time you will wait for protection."

Looking toward the muddy water of the river, Mbula whispered very quietly, "*Muchi wa Kongamato.*"

This story is based on a tradition of the Kaonde, a tribe that lives in northwestern Zambia. The mulendi root paste is a charm used at river crossings for protection against the Kongamato, as reported by a British official named Frank H. Melland. When Melland asked the Kaonde to describe the Kongamato, they at first said it was like a bird. Then they said it was more like a lizard with wings like a bat's. Finally, Melland showed them pictures of various animals, including a prehistoric flying reptile called a pterodactyl. The Kaonde said the pterodactyl looked just like the Kongamato.

Strange flying monsters have been sighted in other areas of Africa, as well as in America and Asia. In the first half of the twentieth century, a sixteen-year-old boy in Namibia claimed to have seen a giant flying snake, and missionaries in Kenya reported "flying dragons." More recent expeditions obtained accounts of flying creatures resembling pterosaurs in both these areas. (Pterosaur is a general term for prehistoric flying reptiles, including the pterodactyl.) In the 1980s there were even reports of pterosaurlike creatures in southern Texas.

In 1932 zoologist Ivan Sanderson was wading across a river in Cameroon, located to the northwest of Zambia, when he was attacked by a horrible black creature with sharp teeth and wings at least twelve feet wide. The native people told him that this was an "Olitiau," and they begged him to leave the area at once. Some researchers believe that the Olitiau and the Kongamato may both be pterosaurs. However, Dr. Sanderson thought the Olitiau was actually a giant carnivorous bat—much larger than any bat known to science. A similar batlike monster called the Ahool has been described by native people on the island of Java in Indonesia.

If the Olitiau and the Ahool are proven to be huge bats, it would be an important scientific discovery. But if the Kongamato is proven to be a living pterosaur, it would be a true scientific breakthrough. The pterosaurs, along with the other dinosaurs, are believed to have died out over 65 million years ago. Could they still exist in the Jiundu swamp of Zambia? Some experts think it is very possible. The Jiundu swamp is similar to the Likouala swamps of the Congo, where Mokele-Mbembe has been sighted (see page 42). Like Mokele-Mbembe, the Kongamato may be a living dinosaur.

Annotated Bibliography

Dinsdale, Tim. *Monster Hunt*. Washington D.C.: Acropolis Books, Ltd., 1972. Originally published as *The Leviathans*, 1966. Dinsdale was one of the most dedicated Loch Ness researchers; contains good illustrations, including stills from his famous film.

Gould, Rupert T. *The Loch Ness Monster and Others*. New York: University Books, 1969. Originally published by Geoffrey Bles, London, 1934. The first serious investigation of the Loch Ness monster; contains many early eyewitness accounts.

Green, John W. *Sasquatch: The Apes Among Us*. Seattle: Hancock House, 1978. The most comprehensive book on the Bigfoot mystery.

Heuvelmans, Bernard. *On the Track of Unknown Animals*. Tr. by Richard Garnett. New York: Hill and Wang, 1959. The classic work by the father of cryptozoology; contains information on all the animals in this book, as well as many others.

International Society of Cryptozoology. *Cryptozoology*. Volumes 1–8, 1982–1989. A scholarly journal published annually; contains research papers, field reports, and laboratory analysis; the best source for current information on cryptozoology.

———. *ISC Newsletter*. 1982–1990. A quarterly newsletter containing up-to-date reports on current research.

Mackal, Roy P. *The Monsters of Loch Ness*. Chicago: The Swallow Press, 1976. A scientific study of the Loch Ness mystery by the foremost American cryptozoologist.

––––––. *Searching for Hidden Animals: An Inquiry into Zoological Mysteries*. Garden City, New York: Doubleday & Company, 1980. Contains chapters on the Giant Octopus, the Kongamato, and the N'yamala (Mokele-Mbembe).

––––––. *A Living Dinosaur? In Search of Mokele-Mbembe*. New York: E. J. Brill, 1987. A fascinating account of Mackal's two expeditions to the Likouala swamps.

Napier, John. *Bigfoot: The Yeti and Sasquatch in Myth and Reality*. New York: E. P. Dutton & Co., 1973. Dr. Napier was an expert on primates; in this book, he expressed belief in the possibility of the Sasquatch (Bigfoot) but was doubtful about the Yeti.

Sanderson, Ivan T. *Investigating the Unexplained: A Compendium of Disquieting Mysteries of the Natural World*. Englewood Cliffs, New Jersey: Prentice-Hall, 1972. Contains four chapters on hidden animals, including the author's personal experience with giant flying creatures.

Shackley, Myra L. *Still Living? Yeti, Sasquatch and the Neanderthal Enigma*. New York: Thames and Hudson, 1983. Contains information on the Almas, Yeti, and Sasquatch, as well as on Chinese and Siberian creatures.

Wood, F. G., and Joseph F. Gennaro, Jr. "An Octopus Trilogy." *National History*, March 1971. Describes the research and scientific analysis that led to identification of the Florida sea monster as a giant octopus.

Wright, Bruce. "The Lusca of Andros." *The Atlantic Advocate*, June 1967. Describes native reports of the Lusca on Andros Island.